IT WORKS!
Revolution in
Communications

John Perritano

 **Marshall Cavendish**
Benchmark
New York

This edition first published in 2010 in the United States
of America by Marshall Cavendish Benchmark.

Marshall Cavendish Benchmark
99 White Plains Road
Tarrytown, NY 10591
www.marshallcavendish.us

Library of Congress Cataloging-in-Publication Data
Perritano, John.
Revolution in communications / by John Perritano.
p. cm. — (It works!)
Summary: "Discusses the history of communication technology, how the technology
was developed, and the science behind it"–Provided by publisher.
Includes bibliographical references and index.
ISBN 978-0-7614-4373-5
1. Telecommunication–
Juvenile literature. I. Title.
TK5102.4.P47 2010
621.382–dc22
2008054347

Cover: Q2AMedia Art Bank
Half Title: Andrew Gray
P7cl: Pictorial Press Ltd/Alamy; P7cr: Bernd Kammerer/Associated Press;
P7bl: Andrew Gray; P11: Photolibrary; P15cl: Julián Rovagnati/
Shutterstock; P15cr: Ronen/Shutterstock; P15br: Ronen/Shutterstock;
P19: Andrea Danti/Shutterstock; P19(inset): Viktor Gmyria/Shutterstock;
P23l: Feng Yu/Shutterstock; P23r: Semisatch/Shutterstock;
P27: Robert Adrian Hillman/Shutterstock; P27: ESA © 2007
Illustrations: Q2AMedia Art Bank

Created by Q2AMedia
Series Editor: Jessica Cohn
Art Director: Sumit Charles
Client Service Manager: Santosh Vasudevan
Project Manager: Shekhar Kapur
Designer: Shilpi Sarkar
Illustrators: Aadil Ahmed, Indranil Ganguly,
Rishi Bhardwaj, Kusum Kala and Sanyogita Lal
Photo research: Shreya Sharma

Printed in Malaysia

135642

Contents

Stop the Presses

Dip! Write! Dip again! Long ago, there was only one way to print a book—by hand. Scribes were people whose job was writing. A scribe would dip the point of a feather into ink. The scribe would write on a piece of **parchment**. When the ink ran dry, the scribe had to dip the writing tool in the ink again.

Printing books this way was long and hard. Only a few books existed. That all changed with German inventor Johannes Gutenberg. He invented the printing press. Gutenberg's invention made it easier to make books.

As a result, more people learned how to read. Soon, people were using the printing press to print newspapers and **pamphlets**. News and ideas could travel faster and farther. The printing press changed the world. Fifty years later, German printers printed more than nine million books.

Meet Johannes Gutenberg

Johannes Gutenberg was born in 1400, in Mainz, Germany. He worked as a goldsmith before becoming a printer. Gutenberg finished his printing press in 1440. He then opened a printing shop in Mainz. It took a while for the printing press to catch on. Other inventors made the printing press better and faster. Gutenberg made a famous book, however. It is called the Gutenberg Bible. He died in 1468. The book is still famous.

My printing press has small metal blocks called type. I can move them around. Each type has a raised letter or number.

I place the letters in rows to form words and sentences. I place the type in the frame of the press.

I then roll ink over the blocks of type. Next, I place a piece of paper over the type. I turn a huge screw that presses the type against the paper.

The ink on the type appears on the paper. A printed page!

Print with a Potato

potato

vegetable brush

carving knife

paper towel

colored marker
(thin point)

black paint

thin aluminum tray

several sheets of
white paper

adult helper

1 Clean a large potato with a vegetable brush. With the help of an adult, use the knife to cut the potato in half.

2 Use the marker to draw a shape onto each half of the potato. The shape could be a star or a happy face. It could be a letter, a number, or even your initials.

3 Using the knife with your adult helper, cut the shape from the potato. Cut the edges so the raised shape stands out.

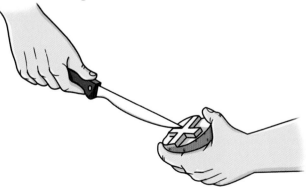

4 Pour paint in the tray. Gently dip the carved potato in the paint. Let the extra paint drip off. Use a paper towel to wipe any drips. Next, press the potato against the paper and watch the image appear.

WHO WOULD HAVE THOUGHT?

E-Books

Book publishing has come a long way since Gutenberg. In fact, publishers no longer need a printing press to publish books. E-books are the wave of the future.

E-Book is short for **electronic** book. All you need to read an e-book is a computer and an Internet connection. Within minutes, you can **download** your favorite books. Most publishers agree that e-books will not take the place of regular books. Yet, e-books are a fun way to read. E-Books allow readers to quickly search for words or phrases. Special devices, called readers, are now available. You can also read an e-book on a **PDA**, or smart phone.

Author Stephen King was one of the first writers to publish an e-book. Readers downloaded 400,000 copies of King's *Riding the Bullet* in the first twenty-four hours it was available.

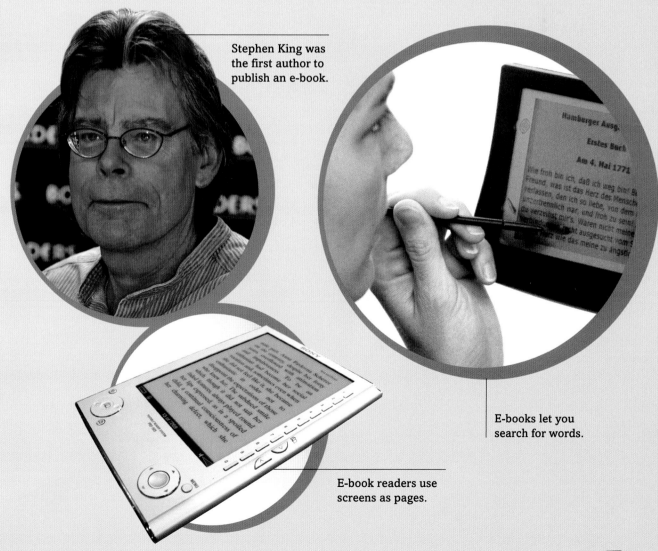

Stephen King was the first author to publish an e-book.

E-books let you search for words.

E-book readers use screens as pages.

Dot . . . Dot . . . Dash—

Long before cell phones, the **telegraph** was the best way to communicate over distances. In 1844, Samuel F. B. Morse opened the first public telegraph line. It ran between Baltimore, Maryland, and Washington, D.C.

Morse's telegraph allowed people to communicate using electronic signals. Those signals were like dots and dashes in a row. A telegraph operator tapped a key at one end of the line. That key turned electricity "on" and "off." Dots were short taps. Dashes were long taps. Morse invented a special code of dots and dashes. An operator could spell out words using the code.

An electrical current sent the dots and dashes through a wire. At the other end was a **receiver.** The first receivers printed out the dots and dashes on paper. It was easier to listen to the dots and dashes, however.

Meet Samuel F. B. Morse

Long before he was a famous inventor, Samuel Morse was an artist. He was a pretty good one. He was born in 1791 and grew up in Massachusetts. Morse liked drawing pictures better than paying attention in class. He traveled to London when he grew up. He studied at the Royal Academy of Art. It was hard for Morse to make a living as a painter, however. At age forty-one, he decided to try being an inventor.

Did you know electricity flows through wire? I can turn on electricity at one end of the wire by tapping a key.

At the other end is a receiver. It has a small spring holding a strip of iron away from an **electromagnet**.

When the electricity is on, the magnet picks up the iron. That produces a sharp click.

What happens when I release the key? Electricity stops flowing to the electromagnet. The spring pulls the iron strip back.

Make an Electromagnet

3-inch (7.5 centimeter) nail

3 feet (1 meter) of coated copper wire from a hardware or electronics store

wire stripper

D-cell battery

electrical tape

several paper clips or thumbtacks

adult helper

1 Have an adult strip 1 inch (2½ cm) of plastic coating off each end of the wire.

2 Wrap most of the wire around the nail. Leave about 8 inches (20 cm) of the wire free at both ends.

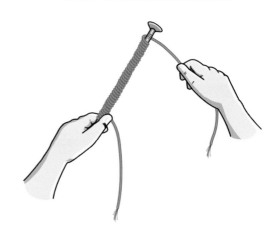

3 Place one end of the wire at one end of the battery. Secure the connection with electrical tape. Repeat with the other end of the wire and the other end of the battery. Just be careful; the wire can start to feel hot.

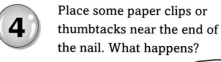

4 Place some paper clips or thumbtacks near the end of the nail. What happens?

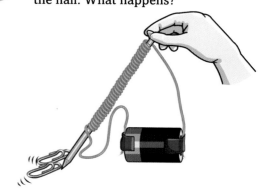

WHO WOULD HAVE THOUGHT?

E-Mail

E-mail is short for electronic mail. The first e-mail was sent in 1971. Ray Tomlinson, an engineer, sent it. He was working on a computer system that would later become the Internet. Scientists built the system so universities could share information.

Tomlinson wanted a better way to leave messages on the computers of other scientists. He needed a way to separate a computer user's address from the name of the **network** the user was on. Tomlinson decided to use the @ sign to do this job. At first, the e-mails people sent were simple word messages. Today, people can send e-mails with pictures and videos.

Can You Hear Me Now?

What was life like before the telephone? People couldn't phone in a pizza order. There were no 911 emergency calls. It was difficult to stay in touch with friends who lived far away.

Alexander Graham Bell saw that it was hard for people to keep in touch. Bell believed he could help them. He thought it was possible to use electricity to send a human voice.

On March 10, 1876, Bell sat in a room with his invention. In another room was Bell's assistant, Thomas Watson. Bell spoke into the mouthpiece. "Mr. Watson, come here!" he said. "I need you."

Watson came running. He had heard Bell! The sound quality wasn't good, but the results were. Their telephone worked.

Meet Alexander Graham Bell

Alexander Graham Bell was born in Edinburgh, Scotland, in 1847. His family moved to Canada in 1870. He moved to Boston, Massachusetts, at age 23. Bell opened a school for teachers of the deaf. At home, he worked on other projects. He wanted to invent a better telegraph machine. At the time, the telegraph was the only way people could communicate over long distances. Bell once told his father that he wanted "friends to converse with each other without leaving home." Bell built something that made that possible. He called his invention the "electrical speech machine." We call it the telephone.

When we speak, the sounds travel as waves through the air.

I talk into my electrical speech machine. A microphone changes those sounds into electrical signals.

Those electrical signals move through wires. The wires connect to a loudspeaker.

The loudspeaker reproduces what I am saying. People can hear me talk.

Mr. Watson, come here! I need you.

13

Sound Travels

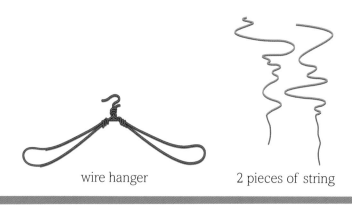

wire hanger

2 pieces of string

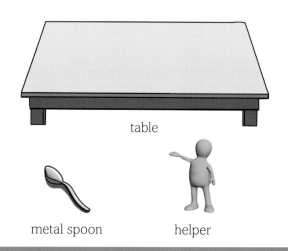

table

metal spoon

helper

1 Tie the end of one string to one end of the hanger. Do the same on the other side.

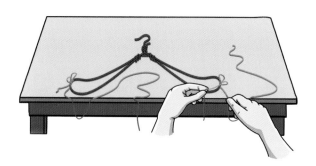

2 Twist each string around your index, or pointing, fingers.

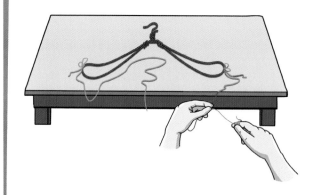

3 Press your fingers to your ears (not "in" your ears).

4 Have your helper tap the hanger on the table. Then ask your helper to tap the hanger with the spoon. What do you hear?

WHO WOULD HAVE THOUGHT?

The Cell Phone

The first telephones were big and clunky. Not anymore! Many people carry cell phones. Most are small enough to fit in your pocket. More than 150 million cell phones are in use. Cell phones are like tiny radios. They send and receive radio signals.

Cell phone networks are divided into "cells." Cells are specific areas. Each cell has a special station that receives and sends radio signals. Each station has an **antenna**. The antenna sends signals just like a radio station does. Your cell phone looks for a signal. Once you're connected, you can talk to friends. You can send **text messages** and photos. Some cell phones even allow you to connect to the Internet, so you can check your messages or visit a website.

All cell phones send voices.

Some cell phones send pictures.

Some cell phones let you type messages.

15

You're on the Air

There's no shortage of radios. They're in the car or at the beach. Some radios are tiny. Others are large. Radios of all sizes have been a big part of life. Not very long ago, people didn't have televisions or MP3s. To hear music or get information, they listened to the radio.

An Italian inventor named Guglielmo Marconi helped make the radio important. Marconi realized that he could send electrical signals by using **radio waves**. He based his ideas on the ideas of others. He knew radio waves occur in nature. These waves cannot be seen. They travel through the air at the speed of light. That's 186,000 miles (299,000 kilometers) per second.

In 1901, Marconi sent a radio signal across the Atlantic Ocean. It went from England to Canada. That made Marconi a star. Soon, people gave Marconi money to start a radio company.

Meet Guglielmo Marconi

Guglielmo Marconi was born in Italy in 1874. His parents were wealthy. The Marconi home had a huge library filled with science books. Marconi was interested in science. By the age of twelve, he was working with wires and batteries. A few years later, he began studying electricity. A German scientist named Heinrich Hertz had discovered radio waves. Marconi knew he was on to something. Marconi believed he could send the dots and dashes of Morse code over those waves. He was right.

IT'S ELECTRIFYING!

A radio has a **transmitter** and a receiver. The transmitter takes a sound and makes it into an electrical current. That current moves up and down. That current is much like a wave on water. I call that movement an audio-**frequency** signal.

Radio stations can broadcast on one frequency. It is called a carrier current. It is the current's job to carry the sound signal. To do that, it changes the signal first.

The carrier current can carry the sound signal to an antenna. There, a radio receiver can pick up the message. The receiver changes the message into something that can be heard.

Radio Waves

portable radio

foil

metal cookie sheet

metal colander
(optional)

1 Tune the radio to a radio station. Try blocking the radio with your hands. Does it stop the sound?

2 Try covering the radio with foil. What happens?

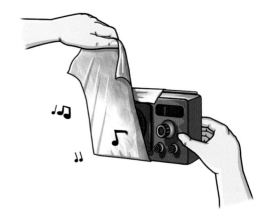

3 Now try blocking the radio waves with the cookie sheet and the colander, if you have one.

4 Metal can block or change signals. Turn on the radio the next time you are in a car. Note if the sound changes when you pass under wires or over metal bridges. What do you hear?

WHO WOULD HAVE THOUGHT?

Satellite Radio

Radio signals break into **static** the farther you get from a radio transmitter. The signal of a **satellite** radio, however, is always clear. Satellite radio can beam high-quality sounds from space directly to your radio. So satellite radio, also known as **digital** radio, is great for sending music.

Satellite radios work in an interesting way. A station on the ground sends a radio signal to a special satellite orbiting Earth. The satellite bounces that signal to your satellite radio receiver. That receiver reads the signal. In addition to sound, that signal also contains other information. It might tell the title of the song and the artist. It might say whether it's hip-hop, jazz, or country music.

Satellite radio can tell you the name of a song.

A special satellite in space directs radio signals to Earth.

Images through the Air

In 1921, Philo Taylor Farnsworth was mowing hay on an Idaho farm. The horse-drawn mower was cutting the grass in lines. Looking at the lines, the fourteen-year-old boy had an idea. Maybe he could make a beam of light draw lines like that. Then he could use light to send moving pictures.

How? He would find a way to scan small lines of an image. He would use the lines as a way to pull the image apart and put it back together. Young Farnsworth drew a picture of his idea for his high school science teacher. Soon, Farnsworth went to college. Then his dad died. The young inventor had to stop going to school. That did not stop him from trying to invent television. At age twenty-one, Farnsworth sent the first TV picture. The picture was just a single black line painted on a piece of glass. Yet it was a start.

Early TV sets were as big as refrigerators, and they cost as much as a new car. The sets had tiny screens. Their images were unclear. Now 99 percent of U.S. households have at least one television. Sixty-six percent of all households have three or more TV sets.

Meet Philo T. Farnsworth

Many inventors worked on ways of sending images through the air. They were somewhat successful. Philo T. Farnsworth, born in 1906, produced the first television image. At the time, only huge machines with spinning discs could produce moving images. Farnsworth's machine had no moving parts. It was simple. The people at RCA, the giant radio company, liked his thinking. They offered Farnsworth money for his invention. While big companies fought for the rights to TV, Farnsworth was largely forgotten. After his death, his role was recognized.

GET THE PICTURE?

I think televisions will run from cameras.

The camera will take an image and break it into tiny points of light. A transmitter will change that light into electrical signals. Those signals can travel through the air on radio waves.

Televisions will grab those signals and change them back into pictures.

Imagine all the things you could put on television.

Make a Stroboscope

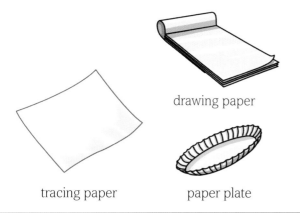

tracing paper   drawing paper   paper plate

mirror

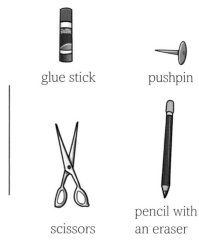

glue stick   pushpin

scissors   pencil with an eraser

1 Cut the edges off the plate. Cut the tracing paper to fit the smaller plate. Draw a car on the notebook paper. Place the tracing paper circle over the car. Draw ten cars in a circle, as shown.

2 Glue the tracing paper to the plate. Cut slits between the cars, as shown.

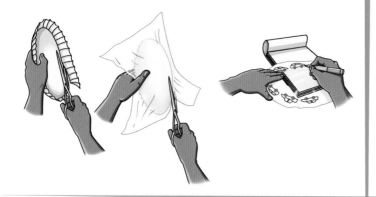

3 Push a pushpin through the plate, in the center of the cars. Hold the eraser to center of the other side of the plate. Push the pin into the eraser. Make sure the circle can spin.

4 Stand in front a mirror. Hold the back of the stroboscope close to your eye. Look through one slit. Spin the circle and watch the cars go!

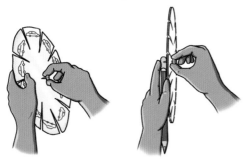

WHO WOULD HAVE THOUGHT?

High-Definition Television

The first television sets were big and bulky. TV shows were broadcast only in black and white. Then color TVs became popular. Now, the newer TVs are HDTVs. *HDTV* stands for High-Definition Television. It also stands for a new way of broadcasting.

What does "high definition" mean? HDTVs can pick up and understand digital signals. HDTVs have more lines per picture than standard TVs. That means you get a much clearer, sharper picture, one that is "highly defined." HDTV screens are also wider and bigger. Watching a high-definition television is a lot like going to the movies. It has awesome images and sound.

Digital television sets can send, store, and change images, just like a computer!

Televisions keep getting flatter.

Older TVs are more like boxes.

World Wide Connection

Whether at home, or at school, or at work, the Internet allows people to get information fast! The Internet is like a huge spiderweb you don't see. You see just the effects! The Web connects millions of computers to one another. The Internet can run on cables or telephone lines. It can run on satellites or radio signals. This system allows people to learn, to have fun, and to communicate with one another.

The idea for the Internet began in the late 1960s. At the time, the U.S. government wanted a special communications system. They called their system **ARPANET**. A few years later, colleges and universities started their own computer network to share information.

In 1989, a British scientist named Tim Berners-Lee changed the way the world used the Internet. He invented **hypertext transfer protocol**, or http. In short, Berners-Lee invented the first Web browser. Finding information fast would soon be only a mouse click away.

THE PLACES YOU'LL GO!

Meet Tim Berners-Lee

Tim Berners-Lee, born in 1955, made the Internet bigger and better. He developed the World Wide Web by creating http. The Web is one of the greatest communication inventions of all time. Because of Berners-Lee, people can watch live TV broadcasts on their computers. They can listen to music, play games, or make telephone calls. They can read magazines and newspapers from other countries.

How does hypertext work? It's simple. It's a way to view text and pictures on your computer.

Every word that is highlighted is linked to more information on another computer.

Log on to the sports page of a newspaper's website. Click on the name of a sports team. The computer jumps to that team's website.

By clicking on these links, you can hopscotch your way through the Internet.

Bits of the Big Picture

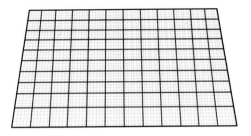

graph paper

colored pencil

 1 To see how TV puts together small parts of a picture, try this. On graph paper, mark off an area 5 blocks high and 5 blocks across. Fill in squares to form a letter. Each square represents one **pixel**.

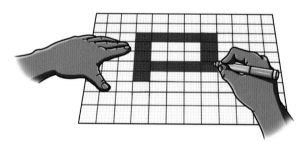

 2 Repeat step 1. This time, work in an area 7 blocks high and 7 blocks wide.

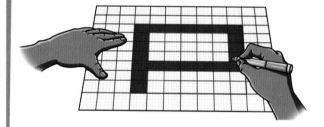

 3 Repeat the step again, working in an area 9 blocks high and 9 blocks wide.

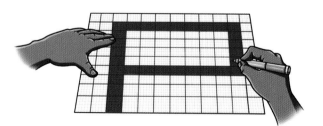

 4 Repeat the process using all the letters of the alphabet. You can even use numbers. How do the letters and numbers compare? Why do you think that is so?

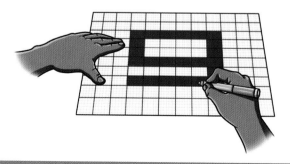

WHO WOULD HAVE THOUGHT?

Webcasts from Mars

The World Wide Web connects information on Earth. Internet users can also connect to outer space. The National Aeronautics and Space Administration (NASA) uses webcasts to connect people to its exploration of Mars.

A webcast is like watching television on your computer. A webcast uses streaming media. Streaming media are sound and moving–picture files. You can download these files over a computer. The webcast can be live. Or it can be recorded for broadcast over the Internet.

Go to http://imaginemars.jpl.nasa.gov/about/webcast.html to view webcasts relating to the Red Planet. Webcasts have become a good tool for learning. NASA and educators use webcasts to teach students.

Timeline

1045
Chinese printer Bi Sheng invents the first movable type out of clay.

1440s
Johannes Gutenberg develops the first printing press with movable type.

1600s
The first newspapers are printed in Europe.

1831
Michael Faraday discovers that sound makes wires vibrate.

1837
Samuel F. B. Morse invents the first usable telegraph machine.

1876
Alexander Graham Bell patents the first telephone.

1989
Tim Berners-Lee invents hypertext links, which make the Internet easier to use.

1969
The U.S. Department of Defense develops ARPANET, which introduced the Internet.

1939
RCA begins the first regular TV broadcasts.

1927
Philo T. Farnsworth transmits moving pictures using his early television.

1901
Italian inventor Guglielmo Marconi sends the first radio communication across the Atlantic Ocean.

Glossary

antenna device that sends or receives electromagnetic waves, such as television and radio signals.

ARPANET computer system developed in the 1960s by the U.S. Department of Defense Advanced Research Projects Agency; formed the basis for the Internet.

digital numerical on-and-off signals, usually in the form of 1s and 0s, that can be read by a computer.

download to copy information from a central computer or online source to another computer.

electromagnet coil of wire around an iron core that acts as a magnet when an electric current flows through the wire.

electronic having to do with electronics, devices powered by controlled electrons.

frequency number of waves within a unit of time.

hypertext transfer protocol (http) series of linked words that allows users to navigate the Internet.

network method of connecting, as in linking computers.

pamphlets thin unbound books.

parchment writing material made out of the skins of animals.

PDA Personal Digital Assistant, a pocket-sized computer device.

pixel basic unit that makes up an image.

radio waves invisible waves that can carry electronic radio signals.

receiver device that can receive signals, such as radio signals.

satellite space vehicle that receives radio, television, and other signals, and relays them back to Earth.

static electrical discharges in the atmosphere that interrupt a radio or television signal.

telegraph electronic system that sends and receives signals in the form of dots and dashes.

text message shortened, typed communication sent via cell phone.

transmitter device that can send signals, such as radio signals.

To Learn More

Books

Guglielmo Marconi and Radio Waves by Susan Zannos. Mitchell Lane Publishers, 2004.

Philo Farnsworth and the Television by Ellen Sturm Niz. Capstone Press, 2006.

Samuel Morse and the Telegraph by David Seidman. Capstone Press, 2007.

Websites

PBS examines the life and works of Alexander Graham Bell. Read a brief biography and follow fascinating links related to the inventor.
http://www.pbs.org/transistor/album1/addlbios/bellag.html

Time magazine offers the online version of its profile of Philo T. Farnsworth, part of the magazine's popular series "Time 100."
http://www.time.com/time/time100/scientist/profile/farnsworth.html

World of Biography offers "Johannes Gutenberg: The Man in Print," a site featuring Gutenberg's achievements.
http://www.worldofbiography.com/9122-Gutenberg/

Index